The Pelican

A Dillon Remarkable Animals Book

The Pelican

By Lynn Stone

DILLON PRESS, INC.
Minneapolis, Minnesota 55415

Photographic Acknowledgments

All photographs in this book are reproduced through the
courtesy of Lynn Stone.

Library of Congress Cataloging-in-Publication Data

Stone, Lynn M.
    The pelican / by Lynn Stone.
        p.   cm. — (A Dillon remarkable animals book)
    Summary: Describes the appearance and behavior of the
pelican and describes its development, life cycles, and range.
    Includes bibliographical references.
    ISBN 0-87518-430-8 (lib. bdg.) : $12.95
    1. Pelicans—Juvenile literature.   2. Pelicans—North
America—Juvenile literature. [1. Pelicans.]
    I. Title.   II. Series.
QL696.P47S75   1990
598.4'3—dc 20   89-26049
                                                            CIP
                                                             AC

Dillon Press, Inc., 242 Portland Avenue South
Minneapolis, Minnesota 55415

Printed in the United States of America
1 2 3 4 5 6 7 8 9 10 99 98 97 96 95 94 93 92 91 90

About the Author

Lynn Stone is a free-
lance writer and photog-
rapher who has written
many natural science
books for young people,
as well as articles for a
variety of national and
regional magazines. His
natural science photo-
graphs have appeared in
a wide range of books
and other publications.
A former teacher, Stone
has taught in public
schools in Illinois and
Florida. He lives with
his family in Batavia,
Illinois.

Contents

Facts about the Pelican

Scientific Name: (White) *Pelecanus erythrorhynchos*
(Brown) *Pelecanus occidentalis*

Related Species: The Australian pelican *(Pelecanus conspicillatus)* in Australia and Tasmania; the Dalmatian pelican *(Pelecanus crispus)* from eastern Europe to China; the great white pelican *(Pelecanus oncrotalus)* in eastern Europe, Asia, and Africa; the grey or spotted-billed pelican *(Pelecanus philippensis)* in southeast India and Sri Lanka; the pink-backed pelican *(Pelecanus rufescens)* in Africa, Madagascar, and Saudi Arabia

Description (White):

Length—5.2 feet (1.6 meters)
Wingspan—8 to 9.5 feet (2.4 to 2.9 meters)
Weight—15 to 20 pounds (6.8 to 9.1 kilograms)
Color—White body; yellowish-orange legs, feet, and pouch; black wingtips
Physical Features—Webbed feet; retractable throat pouch attached to lower, bowed mandible; air sacs located under skin; horn-like growth on upper mandible during breeding season

Description (Brown):

Length—4.2 feet (1.3 meters)
Wingspan—6.5 to 8 feet (2 to 2.4 meters)
Weight—7 to 10 pounds (3.2 to 4.5 kilograms)
Color—Silvery brown body; black feet and legs; blackish-brown pouch becoming reddish or red-tinged during breeding season; head and neck brown and white except for part of

breeding season when head is yellow, neck white

Physical Features—Webbed feet; retractable throat pouch attached to lower, bowed mandible; air sacs located under skin

Distinctive Habits: White pelicans migrate each spring and fall; they often fish cooperatively with flock members herding fish; brown pelicans often fish by making spectacular dives into the sea

Food: White pelicans feed mainly on fish, especially carp, suckers, and other non-game fish; they also eat free-floating salamanders and frogs; brown pelicans eat various species of fish and fish scraps

Reproductive Cycle: In both species, female lays two to three eggs which hatch in about 30 days; time of egg-laying varies with species and location; male and female share duties of hatching and raising young; young fledge and leave nest in about 90 days

Life Span: Captive pelicans have lived for 25 years; 8 to 10 years is an average life span in the wild

Range: White pelicans nest in western and central North America, with small colonies in Texas and Mexico; they winter in the Southeast, California, and Mexico; brown pelicans range along coastal Central America north to British Columbia on the Pacific coast and to North Carolina on the Atlantic coast

Chapter 1

Flying Fishermen

"Closed," the sign on the store read, "Gone Fishing." For pelicans, the big birds with the king-sized pouches, "gone fishing" is a way of life every day. And watching a pelican catch fish is almost as exciting as catching your own.

Diving for Fish

A brown pelican hunting for fish flies 10 to 50 feet (3.1 to 15.2 meters) above the ocean. When it spies fish swimming near the surface, the pelican brakes its flight by pumping its wings and dropping its feet, like airplane flaps. Then, with its wings half folded and its head and neck cocked like a spear, it bolts toward the sea. Splash! A burst of white spray shoots up. For an instant, the pelican disap-

A brown pelican plunges into the sea as it dives for fish.

pears. But suddenly, like a silver and brown cork, it bobs to the surface. Hidden in the pouch under the pelican's lower **mandible***, or bill, are several small fish.

Despite the rough splashdown, the pelican floats on the sea with ease. A few moments later, the long, narrow wings stretch, flap, and lift the pelican swiftly above the waves. The large bird tucks in its feet and climbs skyward, where it joins a small flock of pelicans. The seabirds fly off quickly, yet seldom flap their wings. Their flight is so straight and effortless that they seem to be riding invisible rails in the sky.

Brown pelicans don't always dive for a meal. They also paddle on the sea and plunge their bills into schools of fish. Although several other brown pelicans may be nearby, each one fishes by itself.

Fishing in Flocks

White pelicans are cousins of brown pelicans. They have the same fishing "tackle" as their brown rela-

*Words in **bold type** are explained in the glossary at the end of this book.

After diving, a brown pelican rises swiftly from the water.

tives, but they have a different method for catching
fish. White pelicans may fish alone, but they usually
fish in flocks. A flock of white pelicans paddles in a
broad line, herding fish ahead through the water.
Soon the pelicans begin to make a circle around the
fish, trapping their **prey** in the center of the flock.
Then the birds dip their pouches like nets into the

White pelicans fish in flocks, working together to catch their food.

school of fish. If a fish darts away from one pouch, it is likely to be scooped up by another. Scientists call this type of hunting *cooperative* or *communal*, because the birds work together. White pelicans are among the few animals that hunt cooperatively.

Pelicans feed on various sizes and kinds of fish. A pelican could hold a fish weighing several pounds

12

in its pouch and probably swallow it whole. But normally it catches several small fish in a mouthful rather than large fish one at a time. In Florida, brown pelicans have been known to eat 30 different types of saltwater fish.

Pelicans are wonderfully suited for flying, swimming, and fishing. But on the ground, sitting and walking, they do not look like sleek, graceful, long-winged fliers.

At close range a pelican is a curious sight. It has almost no tail, and its legs are stubby. Its feet are broad and webbed, like those of a duck. When it walks, it waddles. Its neck is long and so, too, is its bill. A pelican often tilts the bill against its neck. When the bird shifts its eyes without lifting the bill, it looks like someone trying to peer over spectacles.

The pelican is well suited for fishing because it has the proper tackle. The webbed feet are the pelican's paddles. It does not need long legs for wading, but it does need to swim. The pelican's eyes provide excellent eyesight. Flying over water, it has to be

able to see its swiftly moving prey.

Another important part of the pelican's fishing tackle is its **plumage**, or covering of feathers. The feathers are kept tidy because a pelican takes great care to **preen**. A pelican preens when it uses its bill to clean, straighten, and oil its feathers. The body oil that a pelican applies waterproofs its feathers. With this protection, the pelican floats easily and does not become waterlogged. Water beads in droplets on pelican feathers, just as it does on a freshly waxed car.

Along with waterproofing, webbed feet, and sharp eyes, pelicans have hollow bones. Hollow bones help keep a pelican light enough to fly. Very few of the world's flying birds weigh more than a male white pelican. But for its size, the big bird is a lightweight.

The ability to fly helps a pelican reach its favorite fishing spot. Air sacs help it when it lands on or dives into the water. Both brown and white pelicans have air sacs under their skin that help the

On land, a pelican does not look like a graceful flying bird.

A brown pelican preens feathers on its wing.

birds float. In the case of the brown pelican, they help cushion dives.

A Remarkable Pouch
The pelican's most well known fishing tackle is its remarkable throat pouch. The pouch is made of

skin which stretches like a balloon. When the pelican chooses, it stores the pouch in its lower mandible. As the pouch fills with water, it stretches into the familiar bag shape.

The pelican's lower mandible is like a long, narrow hoop. The pouch is attached to it and hangs below it. When the pouch fills, the sides of the lower mandible bow outward into a rounder hoop. The mandible closes to its normal shape as the water drains out.

People once believed that pelicans stored fish in their pouches. Some thought that the birds kept water in the pouch to keep the fish alive, as if the pouch were a flying aquarium. Certainly a pelican's pouch could hold fish for a long period of time, but it does not. A pelican stores fish only in its stomach, not in its pouch.

For the pelican, the pouch is a soft-sided fish scoop. It can hold from 2 to 3 gallons (7.6 to 11.4 liters) of water and is more than 6 inches (15 centimeters) deep.

A brown pelican swallows fish from its pouch.

The pouch also helps a pelican cool off on hot days. A pelican at rest can flutter its open pouch up to 250 times per minute. The bird makes this rapid movement by using the *U*-shaped bones at the base of its tongue and special muscles. The fluttering releases heat through the bare skin of the pouch.

When it is resting, the pelican can move its

The lower mandible of this white pelican is bowed outward into the shape of a round hoop while the pelican eats the fish it has scooped up in its pouch.

19

Spreading its lower mandible, this brown pelican has turned its amazing pouch inside out.

pouch in an amazing way. You have probably turned a sock inside out. Imagine turning the skin at the bottom of your mouth inside out. Your throat skin is not long or loose enough to turn up and out, but the pelican's pouch is. With its head against its shoulders and its neck *S*-curved under its

20

bill, the pelican spreads the lower mandibles. It pushes the bottom of the pouch against the bend of its neck. The pouch is turned inside out for about two seconds.

The pelican may follow that exercise with another strange movement. It tosses its head skyward, stretching its neck and pouch to full length. For a moment, it looks like an alien animal! The large bird probably performs these movements for its comfort, just as a person might stretch or yawn.

Pelicans are indeed fascinating animals. The bird's long bill, stubby legs, and wonderful pouch are important parts of its natural tackle box. For the pelican, fishing is serious business.

Chapter 2

In Brown and White

In North America, wild pelicans may be brown pelicans or white pelicans. Like all living creatures, each **species**, or kind, of pelican has been given its own name by scientists. The American white pelican is known among the world's **ornithologists**, scientists who study birds, as *Pelecanus erythrorhynchos*. The brown pelican is called *Pelecanus occidentalis*.

This book is about the North American species of pelicans. In addition to the two North American species, there are five or six other species of pelicans. They all live in the warmer regions of the world. Some ornithologists believe that the brown pelicans of Peru are a separate species. In many ways they are unlike the brown pelicans of North America.

In December in Florida, a brown pelican has acquired its early breeding plumage.

23

All of the pelicans belong to a larger group of birds called Pelecaniformes. Among them are tropic-birds, gannets, cormorants, anhingas, frigatebirds, and boobies. Pelecaniformes have fully webbed feet and throat pouches. None of them, however, has a pouch the size of a pelican's.

Different Colors and Sizes

Although brown and white pelicans are closely related, they are also different in some ways. The most obvious difference lies in their plumage. The white pelican is white with a colorful trim. Its wing-tips are black, and its pouch and feet are a mix of yellow and orange. It may have a few yellowish feathers on its breast and forehead, and a showy crest in spring.

Brown pelicans may be divided into three or four varieties, or subspecies. Each group of brown pelicans is somewhat different from the others. Yet it is not different enough to make up a separate species of pelican. All brown pelicans, as adults,

A white pelican in breeding plumage.

have silvery brown bodies. The color of their necks, eyes, heads, and pouches changes greatly with the seasons. A Florida brown pelican, for example, may have a white neck in December and a brown neck with a yellow "vest" in March. Meanwhile, its head changes from bright yellow to white.

White pelicans are larger than their brown cousins. White pelicans weigh from 15 to 20 pounds (6.8 to 9.1 kilograms) and have wingspans as wide as 9.5 feet (2.9 meters). California brown pelicans weigh from 8 to 10 pounds (3.6 to 4.5 kilograms) and have wingspans from 7 to 8 feet (2.1 to 2.4 meters). They are slightly larger than the brown pelicans of eastern North America. The males of both species are about one-third larger than the females.

Habitat and Range

Another difference between the pelicans is their choice of **habitat**. Brown pelicans live along the sea-coasts. They feed in the oceans and **estuaries**,

Brown pelicans feed in the surf along the Florida coast.

where fresh water from rivers flows into the salt water of the oceans. Sometimes brown pelicans stray a few miles inland. Usually, though, they remain around salt or **brackish** water, which is a blend of fresh water and seawater.

The area in which an animal can be found is

its **range**. The huge range of the brown pelican along the Pacific coast stretches from southern British Columbia in Canada to southern Chile in South America. Along the Atlantic coast, brown pelicans can be found from North Carolina south to Guyana in northern South America. In western North America, brown pelicans nest on offshore islands from southern Mexico north to southern California. Brown pelicans along the Atlantic coast of North America nest on coastal islands from North Carolina south to Florida, Texas, and the Caribbean Sea.

White pelicans spend much of their lives in a freshwater habitat. Most white pelicans nest on islands in lakes of the western United States and western Canada. Nesting, or **breeding**, white pelicans are more plentiful in Canada than in the United States. **Colonies** are found in the provinces of Saskatchewan, Alberta, Manitoba, Ontario, and British Columbia. White pelicans in the United States nest in North Dakota, South Dakota, Mon-

A nesting colony of white pelicans in Montana.

tana, Utah, Wyoming, California, Colorado, Nevada, Minnesota, Oregon, and Texas.

The Texas colony is one of only two white pelican colonies surrounded by salt water. The other lies on the gulf coast of Mexico.

The southernmost colony of nesting white

29

pelicans is found at Lago de Santiaguillo, a fresh-water lake near Durango, Mexico. This colony lies 4,000 miles (6,440 kilometers) from the large white pelican colonies in Canada. The Lago de Santiaguillo colony is the only colony of white pelicans known to nest in the winter. This flock is also unusual because, like the other colonies of Mexico and Texas, it does not **migrate** long distances. The huge white pelican flocks of Canada and other areas of the United States do travel great distances. Each spring they leave southern coasts and migrate north to their nesting territories. Each autumn they make the return flight south.

Although they spend the winter months along seacoasts, white pelicans do not fish in the open sea. They like the quiet waters of bays and estuaries. Most white pelican flocks spend the winter along the coasts of California, Mexico, Texas, and Florida. Because of their different choices in habitat, brown and white pelicans rarely compete for food. Sometimes they do share the same sand bar for a rest.

White and brown pelicans share a sand bar.

At Home with Gulls

Pelicans are more likely to share time and space with gulls than with pelicans of another species. Gulls nest among the white pelican colonies. But if adult pelicans leave their nests, gulls eat pelican eggs and newborn babies. Why would pelicans live with such threatening neighbors? Pelicans are

31

rather gentle birds. Despite their great size, they pose no threat to the gulls. And perhaps the gulls' presence is of some benefit to the pelicans. Gulls are loud, bold birds. Their ability to drive away other animals from the nesting area helps protect pelican nests as well as gull nests.

Gulls often follow brown pelicans on their seaside hunts. When a brown pelican crashes headlong into the sea and bobs up, a gull may be nearby. Like a pirate, a gull may land on a pelican's head in hopes of snatching a fish. Gulls have learned that fish sometimes slip away as the pelican drains water from its pouch.

In search of an easy meal, a gull perches on the head of a brown pelican.

Chapter 3

The Pelican's Year

For pelicans, the busiest time of year is the nesting season. The nesting of brown and white pelicans often takes place at different times and at widely scattered places. Still, the major events of the nesting season are much alike for both species.

Pelican flocks, ranging in size from two or three dozen to several thousand, settle onto islands. Usually the flocks return to a place where they have nested before. The birds select mates and build nests. They lay eggs and **incubate** them at a certain temperature for about 30 days. Then the parents, male and female, spend nearly three months feeding their growing chicks. By that time the young pelicans, usually no more than one per nest, are full grown and strong enough to fly.

A brown pelican parent watches over its chick in a nest on a mangrove island.

Brown pelicans nest on an island of mangroves along Florida's gulf coast.

A Nesting Colony

One nesting colony of brown pelicans lies near Sarasota along Florida's southern gulf coast. Each February hundreds of brown pelicans gather on little coastal islands made of mangroves. Mangroves are low, bushy trees that grow in shallow saltwater bays and lagoons. There the trees are sheltered from the large waves of the open ocean.

The islands are ideal for pelicans and other water birds. Because they are surrounded by water, they protect the birds from **predators** such as dogs, bobcats, and most snakes. And since the islands are close to the sea, the pelicans can fish nearby.

By February the weather has become quite warm. The pelicans sense that it is time to begin nesting. Their plumage is splendid. Both males and females have white necks and yellow heads. Their eyes become light-colored and ringed by red.

The pelicans usually nest in the outermost branches of the mangroves. That way they can spread their wings and spring into the air without crashing through branches. Big, long-legged wading birds, such as great egrets and great blue herons, share the outer branches with the pelicans. Double-crested cormorants perch on the top, outer branches. Several smaller birds—black crowned night herons and snowy egrets among them—nest in the dark tangles of inner branches. Together,

These brown pelicans share a mangrove nesting colony with a great egret and double-crested cormorants.

the birds keep up a steady chorus of grunts, croaks, and squeals.

Not all brown pelicans begin their annual nesting in February. The brown pelicans of the Carolinas do not begin nesting until spring. Brown pelicans in the Caribbean Sea and Florida Keys may nest at any time of year. California brown pelicans, like those along Florida's gulf coast, begin nesting in February.

Once they have settled among the trees, each male brown pelican sets up a small territory in the branches. A male uses gestures, or body movements, to attract a mate. He does not sing or call. After much bowing, stretching, and displaying of his pouch, the male gains the attention—and affection—of a female.

Having taken a mate, the male brown pelican carries small branches to the female. She constructs a nest of sticks in the tree. In other colonies, brown pelicans nest in a variety of places. Sometimes they nest in fairly tall trees. They may also use low bushes or nest on the ground.

After two weeks in the mangroves, the pelican pair has a completed nest. The female lays two or three chalk-colored eggs, each twice the size of hen's eggs. She and the male take turns sitting on the eggs to keep them warm.

Meanwhile, several other brown pelicans have begun incubating within outstretched wings of each other. None of the pelicans seems to mind this togetherness. In fact, pelicans seem to enjoy each other's company. Still, when one pelican steps too close to the nest of another, the nesting bird will jab with its bill at the trespasser.

White Pelican Nests

White pelicans begin to prepare for nesting early in the spring. Males and females develop long, fancy feathers called plumes on their heads, and a mysterious "horn" on their upper mandible. This hornlike growth is temporary. It may be 4 inches (10 centimeters) tall before it drops off in June, when the young hatch. Ornithologists are not sure what the purpose of the growth is.

White pelicans arrive on their nesting islands in western lakes in April. The ice and snow have just recently melted away. For two weeks the white pelicans choose nesting sites and mates. The

A white pelican in breeding plumage has a "horn" on its upper mandible.

females usually lay eggs in early May. Most white pelican nests are shallow holes in the soil or low platforms of sticks. A few colonies nest on floating mats of water plants.

White pelican eggs hatch in early June. The pelican babies, both white and brown, hatch with the help of a special "egg tooth." This sharp growth on the upper mandible helps the baby chip a hole in the egg. Bit by bit, the chick widens the hole and cracks the egg open.

Pelican Babies

Brown and white pelicans raise their young in similar ways. Although most pelican nests contain two or three eggs, adult pelicans usually raise just one baby. Pelican eggs hatch two or three days apart. The first-born chick is larger and stronger than the one born later. This makes it possible for the larger chick to take most of the food brought by the parents. More often than not, it will peck and push its smaller brother or sister from the nest.

A newborn white pelican.

Adult pelicans rarely try to stop these family fights. The bigger, stronger first baby survives. The younger one starves to death or dies from being exposed to too much sunlight or cold air.

Why would pelicans "waste" an egg or two? Ornithologists believe pelicans are making sure that one of their babies will live to become full grown. If the first egg fails or the chick dies, there is a second egg and sometimes a third. When food is plentiful, the adults may raise two young or, rarely, three.

A baby pelican is born with bare skin and tiny, flipperlike wings. At about eight days of age, it can hold its head upright. A few days later, it begins to develop a coat of soft, fuzzy feathers called **down**.

Usually, the presence of an adult pelican at the nest keeps predators away. If both parents leave the nest for any reason, eggs and newborn chicks are easy prey for gulls, crows, vultures, or ravens.

Baby pelicans lead sheltered lives for their first three to four weeks. They are very sensitive to heat and cold. Parents protect them from the weather by **brooding**—keeping the young pelicans tucked under their feathers. As the babies' own feathers grow, they begin to protect the chicks against cold and heat. Then the parents do not have to brood them all the time.

This brown pelican chick has started to develop a coat of warm down feathers.

Pelican chicks need their parents' attention from the time of birth until they can fly, 10 to 12 weeks later. The babies eat only what their parents bring to them. They have no way of catching fish or defending themselves.

A newborn pelican is fed small bits of fish by its parents. Adult pelicans **regurgitate** part of the fish they catch when they return to their nest. The partly digested food, little more than smelly fish soup, oozes from the adult's bill.

Soon, however, the chick is old enough to sit up and feed from the adult's pouch. At feeding time, the young pelican is loud and demanding. While the parent pumps food from its stomach into its throat and pouch, the chick pecks at the adult's pouch. After it is several weeks old, a chick nearly topples its parents when it feeds. Adult pelicans sometimes have a hard time shaking their hungry baby out of their mouths. By the time a young pelican can fly, it will probably have eaten from 150 to 200 pounds (68 to 91 kilograms) of fish.

A large white pelican chick feeds from its parent's pouch.

As it grows, a chick begins to explore. A baby brown pelican in a tree cannot move very far. It does manage to climb about near its nest. Young white pelicans form flocks of down-covered birds that waddle around the nesting island together. Somehow, each chick can identify its parents when one or the other returns from a fishing trip.

Ready to Fly and Fish

By three months of age, a young pelican's wings are fully developed. The young pelican has exercised its wings daily, and now it has **fledged**—it can fly.

Young pelicans usually weigh more than adults when they make their first solo flights. The extra body fat is important because young pelicans do not yet have their parents' fishing skills. If necessary, they can live on their fat for several days. Still, many of the birds die during their first year, often the result of not having mastered fishing skills.

After the nesting season, both adult and newly-fledged Florida brown pelicans do not travel far from their nests. Brown pelicans in other regions, though, travel long distances after nesting. California brown pelicans, for example, fly in large numbers from California and Mexico north along the Pacific shore. Carolina-born brown pelicans migrate south to Florida.

Pelicans of all species are warm weather birds. White pelicans, except those in Texas and Mexico, migrate south after the nesting season. By mid-fall great flocks of white pelicans pass like clouds of snowflakes through southern skies.

Young pelicans join in flocks mixed with adults of various ages. Brown pelicans are nearly five years old before they look like adults. People often mistake the young pelicans, in their dull brown plumage, for a different kind of bird. Young white pelicans have a gray bill, pouch, and cap. Both species may be five years old before they are ready for their own nests.

Like the older adults, these young pelicans spend their remaining summer and fall days fishing, resting on sand bars, and preening. At sunset they fly to a **roost** on an island, where they rest at night. Each morning at dawn, they head for a favorite fishing place.

Chapter 4

Pelicans and People

Not all pelicans begin their day with a swim. In fact, some brown pelicans on both coasts, especially in California and Florida, depend on people for food. They stay near docks where fishermen provide them with fish.

Dangerous Fish Hooks and Line

Unfortunately, the brown pelicans' willingness to mix with people is often deadly. The pelicans sometimes die when the bones of cleaned fish stick in their throats. More often, the birds become caught on fish hooks or line that a fisherman has thrown away. Fishermen reel in pelicans that attack their bait fish. Some say that pelicans they have caught have a dozen rusting fish hooks in their bills.

On the Florida coast, a brown pelican perches on a rock close to a fisherman.

Searching for fish, a group of brown pelicans waits near two fishermen.

Pelicans are protected by laws in Mexico, Canada, and the United States. Still, fishermen sometimes kill them. A few people think of pelicans as pests that catch their fish. One fisherman in California complained that when he fished, "there could be hundreds of pelicans around the boat. You have to throw a bunch of anchovies over one side to distract them. Then you throw out your line on the other side."

Brown pelicans and people pose some problems for each other. But the big bird's ability to live and nest in areas where many people live has probably helped it survive.

Danger from DDT

In the late 1960s, the brown pelican was in serious trouble in the United States. Chemicals such as DDT were once used to control insects. In time, the chemicals washed from land into the sea. Tiny animals took them into their bodies. These creatures were eaten by larger animals, such as fish, which also became carriers of the harmful chemicals. Pelicans that fed on the fish began to lay eggs with thin shells. The chemicals from DDT affected the birds' ability to lay normal eggs. When the pelicans tried to incubate, the eggs broke under their weight. In California, Louisiana, Texas, and South Carolina, the brown pelicans began to disappear.

They became an **endangered species.**

In 1972, the U.S. Environmental Protection Agency banned almost all uses of DDT. Brown pelicans now have nesting colonies again in Texas, Louisiana, South Carolina, and California. The Florida birds, which were not exposed to much DDT, have maintained their numbers. Brown pelicans are no longer endangered in the United States.

White pelicans were not hurt badly by DDT, either. Now, with added protection for their nesting areas, their numbers seem to be growing. There are 125,000 white pelicans in North America. The brown pelican population, including those in Central America and Mexico, is much larger. Ornithologists are not sure what the total is.

Pelicans still have problems. Overfishing of lakes and seas by people reduces the fish available to birds. Power boats upset nesting colonies. Water pollution and the poisoning of fish hurt pelicans. When people change the natural water levels in lakes, that hurts pelicans, too. High water

Once endangered in many areas, brown pelicans are once again nesting and raising chicks.

can flood nests or make fish hard to catch. Low water can kill fish and open land bridges to what had been islands.

Help for Pelicans

Still, the number of people who appreciate pelicans and other wild animals is growing. The first

national wildlife refuge in the United States was established in 1903 by President Theodore Roosevelt. This special place helped protect brown pelicans and other animals that lived within it. Today, brown and white pelicans are protected in dozens of wildlife refuges in the United States and Canada. Injured pelicans are helped by many people. A number of zoos and animal care centers treat and house pelicans that are injured and cannot be returned to the wild.

One of the best places to see pelicans being helped is at Ralph Heath's Suncoast Seabird Sanctuary in Indian Shores, Florida. Many injured pelicans nest at the sanctuary and raise healthy babies.

Pelicans are raising healthy chicks in the wilds of North America, too. If we take care to protect pelicans and their habitat, these remarkable flying fishermen will continue to enrich the natural beauty of our lakes, seas, and skies.

In many ways, the actions of people will affect the future of the pelican.

Glossary

brackish (BRAHK-ish)—a blend of salt water and fresh water

breeding—used here to mean the season when animals mate and produce young

brooding—keeping a young bird warm and dry by tucking it under an adult's feathers

colony—used here to mean a group of animals gathered together to nest or breed

down—used here to mean the soft, fuzzy feathers produced by baby birds

endangered species (en-DANE-jerd SPEE-sheez)—a kind of animal that is in danger of extinction, or disappearing from the earth

estuary (EST-u-airy)—the mouth of a river where it meets the sea

fledge—to reach flying age

habitat—the particular kind of area where a plant or animal naturally lives within a larger area

incubate (INK-u-bate)—to keep eggs warm until they hatch

mandible—the upper or lower section of a jaw or bird's bill

migrate—to move with changing seasons from one area or climate to another for feeding or breeding

ornithologist (ohr-nuh-THAHL-uh-jihst)—a scientist who studies birds

plumage (PLOO-midj)—a bird's covering of feathers

predator (PREHD-uh-tuhr)—an animal that hunts other animals for food

preen—to use the beak to clean and straighten feathers

prey—an animal that is hunted by another animal for food

range—the geographic area in which an organism, or living thing, is found

regurgitate (re-GUR-jih-tate)—to bring partially digested food up from the stomach into the mouth

roost—the place where a bird rests

species (SPEE-sheez)—one kind of animal within a group of several closely related kinds; brown and white pelicans are both species

Index